Slam Dunk for Mark

Written by
Rob Waring and **Maurice Jamall**

Before You Read

be sick (not well)

to cook

to throw

basketball team

cup

dinner

7:00 PM

doctor

finals

BILL MASTERSON CUP
CHAMPIONSHIP
MATCH
BAYVIEW ⊻ NEWTOWN

grandma → grandmother

vegetable soup

busy

In the story

Mark

Mark's grandmother

Anthony

"Give me the ball, Mark!" shouts Anthony.
Today is a big basketball game. Bayview High School is playing Newtown High School.
Both teams are very good. Newtown High is winning. Mark and Anthony play for Bayview High. Mark is Bayview's star player.

The game is very exciting. There is only a little more time. The score is 75 points to Newtown High, and 74 points to Bayview High.

The Newtown player throws the ball, but Mark stops it. Bayview High has one more minute to win the game. . .

Mark has the ball now. He goes around one player, and another.
He jumps and . . . it's a slam dunk! Two points for Bayview!
Bayview High wins the game!
Bayview High can go to the finals tomorrow afternoon.
"Bayview! Bayview! Bayview!" shout the Bayview High students.

"Great play, Mark!" says Anthony.
The basketball team is very happy with Mark.
"Great job, Mark!" says his team.
"Thanks! Good game everybody!" says Mark.
"Good game, everybody. We'll win the cup tomorrow!" he says.

Mark's teacher, Mr. Harris, says, "Good job, Mark, and good luck in tomorrow's game. With you on the team, we'll win the cup again!"

"Thanks, Mr. Harris. Yes, we'll win," says Mark. "We have a good team. We'll win!"

Mark gets home. He usually gets home at 6 o'clock, but today his grandmother is sick again. It's now 4 o'clock that afternoon.

"I'm home, Grandma," he says.

Mark lives with his grandmother. He loves her very much. He has no mother and no father. His grandmother is very old, and sometimes she is not well.

"Grandma," he says. "Are you okay?"

"Hello, Mark." she says. "No, I'm sick again. But tell me about your basketball game. Is your team playing in the finals, Mark?" she asks.

"Yes, we are," he replies. "We're in the finals now. The game is tomorrow afternoon."

His grandmother says, "The finals? Really? That's great, Mark." She is very happy for Mark. She smiles at him.

Mark likes to make dinner for his grandmother.
He asks, "What do you want for dinner, Grandma?"
"Let's have a nice vegetable soup," she says.
Mark says, "That's a good idea. Okay, I'll make that."
She says, "Thank you, Mark. You're very good to me."
"You wait there, Grandma," he says.

Mark gets dinner ready. He likes cooking.
He often cooks for his grandmother. And he always cooks when his grandmother is sick.
He makes vegetable soup, a salad, and many other things.
Mark is a very good cook.
"Grandma, dinner's ready," he says.

Mark looks at his grandmother. He is worried about her.
"Let's go to the doctor tomorrow after school," he says.
She says, "Thank you, Mark. But you have a basketball game
tomorrow. I want you to play. You never miss a game."
"I know, Grandma. But I'm not worried about the game," he
says. "I'm worried about you. I'll take you to the doctor's."

At school the next morning, Anthony says to Mark, "We'll win this afternoon, Mark. With you on the team, we'll win the cup." He is very excited.

"I can't play this afternoon," says Mark.

Anthony is really surprised. "What? You can't play! Why?"

"I'm busy this afternoon," says Mark.

"Busy?" says Anthony. "Busy! But, you're never too busy for basketball! And it's the finals."

"I'm sorry, I can't play," says Mark.

Everybody in school is angry with Mark. He always plays in the finals, but he will not play that afternoon. They want the school to win the cup.

They do not know about his sick grandmother. Mark does not want to tell them about her.

"He's too busy," says Anthony to his friend, Mike.

"Listen, I *am* busy this afternoon. I'm sorry," Mark says.

But nobody listens to Mark. They all want him to play. They do not understand him.

At lunchtime, Mark wants to sit with his friend, Gemma.
He goes to Gemma's table.

"You can't sit here!" she says to Mark.

"Excuse me?" says Mark. "Why?"

"Only my *friends* can sit here," Gemma says. "And *you* are not my friend."

Nobody wants to sit with Mark. Nobody wants to eat with him. They are angry. They want him to play. Mark is very sad.

Later that afternoon is the big game. But Mark is not playing basketball. He is with his grandmother at the doctor's.

"Thank you for coming with me, Mark," says his grandmother.

"That's okay, Grandma," he says. "I want to be here. You'll be well soon. You're very important to me. And basketball is only a game."

"Sometimes, people don't understand that," he says.